What's in this book

This book belongs to

T0351530

_____

我们都一样 We are the Same

学习内容 Contents

沟通 Communication

说说五官

Talk about parts of the face

背景介绍：
小朋友们来自不同的国家、地区和种族，有不同的肤色、发色和五官长相等等，但大家都是人类大家庭中的一员，人人都是地球上的一份子。

生词 New words

★ 头	head
★ 耳朵	ear
★ 眼睛	eye
★ 鼻子	nose
★ 嘴巴	mouth
这	this
是	to be
的	of

这是我的头。
This is my head.

这是他的嘴巴。
This is his mouth.

这是她的鼻子。
This is her nose.

跨学科学习 Project

认识视觉、听觉、嗅觉、味觉
及相应的器官
Learn about the senses and the
corresponding parts of the face

文化 Cultures

中国的眼保健操
Chinese eye exercises

参考答案：
1 Three/All of my friends have black hair.
2 We might look different to each other, but we all have a head,
   a nose, a mouth, two eyes and two ears.
3 I like my eyes/mouth most.

Get ready

1 How many of your friends have black hair?

2 How are we different? How are we the same?

3 Which part of the face do you like most?

故事大意：
我们不一样，因为我们来自不同的国家、地区和种族，有不同的长相。
我们都一样，因为我们都是人类，脸部结构都相同。

tóu
头

这是我的头。

参考问题和答案：

1　What is the boy pointing to? (He is pointing to his head.)

2　Do you have a head? (Yes, I do.)

 4　3　Do your friends also have a head? (Yes, they do.)

ěr duo

耳朵

这是我的耳朵。

参考问题和答案：

1 What is the girl touching? (She is touching her ear.)
2 Do you have ears? (Yes, I do.)
3 Do your friends also have ears? (Yes, they do.)

yǎn jing

眼睛

这是他的眼睛。

参考问题和答案：

1 What can you see through the magnifying glass? (I can see the boy's eye.)

2 Do you have eyes? (Yes, I do.)

3 Do your friends also have eyes? (Yes, they do.)

bí zi
鼻子

这是她的鼻子。

参考问题和答案：

1 What can you see through the magnifying glass? (I can see the girl's nose.)
2 Do you have a nose? (Yes, I do.)
3 Do your friends also have a nose? (Yes, they do.)

zuǐ ba

嘴巴

这是我们的嘴巴。

参考问题和答案：

1 What is the baby pointing to? (She is pointing to her mouth.)

2 Do you have a mouth? (Yes, I do.)

3 Do your friends also have a mouth? (Yes, they do.)

我们不一样，我们都一样。

参考问题和答案：

1 How are the children different? (They come from different countries and areas, and are of different races, so they look different to each other.)
2 How are the children the same? (They are all human beings. They all have a head, two ears, two eyes, a nose and a mouth.)

Let's think

1 Look carefully. Circle the parts of the child's face.

通过提问来引导学生找到正确答案。如："这个小朋友的眼睛是大还是小？"
"他的鼻子上有雀斑吗？""他是张着嘴巴还是闭着嘴巴？"

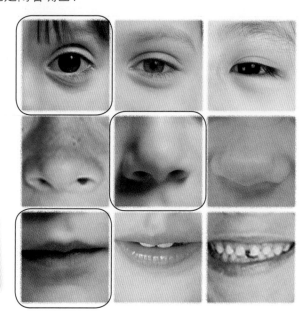

2 Look at the pictures and listen to your teacher. Put a tick or a cross.

1 　　这是她的嘴巴。　　✗

2 　　这是他的耳朵。　　✗

3 　　这是她的鼻子。　　✓

New words

1 Learn the new words.

头

眼睛

鼻子

耳朵

嘴巴

这是我的。

2 Draw arrows to label the clown's face. Colour the balloons.

头

眼睛

鼻子

耳朵

嘴巴

延伸活动：
老师或一名学生随意指向自己的脸部器官，其他学生说出该器官名称。

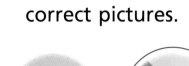

1 Listen and circle the correct pictures.

2 Look at the pictures. Listen to the st

1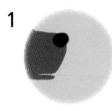

2

3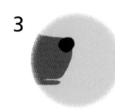

4

①

这是我和姐姐。我们的鼻子一样。

③

我们的眼睛、鼻子和耳朵都一样。

Which two of the children look the same in the story? (Ethan and Ivan.)

Do you have any brothers or sisters? Do you look the same or different? (I have a twin brother. We look the same./I have a sister. Our eyes look similar, but our noses and mouths are different.)

say.

第三题录音稿：

1 这是爱莎。这是她的耳朵和嘴巴。

2 这是我的弟弟。这是他的耳朵和眼睛。

3 这是伊森的眼睛。

4 这是我。这是我的鼻子和嘴巴。

 3 Listen and circle the correct parts of the face.

1

2

3

4

4 Talk with your friend.

参考对话：

A：这是我的鼻子。

B：这是我的眼睛。

Task

学生可以贴一张自己的家人或宠物的照片。

Paste your photo and talk about it.

这是我的小狗。

这是我的爸爸和妈妈。
这是我的弟弟。

这是我的姐姐。她叫
依依。她十岁。

Paste your photo here.

参考画法：
1 他有鼻子和耳朵。
2 他有眼睛和嘴巴。
3 他有眼睛、鼻子和嘴巴。

Game

Listen to your teacher and draw the monsters' faces.

可让学生发挥创意，自行决定怪兽脸部器官的位置和数量。

Song

学生一边唱歌，一边配合歌词指向自己的脸部器官。

 **Listen and sing.**

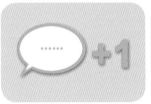

头、眼睛、耳朵、鼻子、嘴巴。

头、眼睛、耳朵、鼻子、嘴巴。

我们有眼睛、耳朵、鼻子、嘴巴，

我们都一样呀，都一样。

课堂用语 Classroom language

再说一遍。	再读一遍。	再来一次。	跟我读。
Say it again.	Read it again.	And again.	Read after me.

写一写 Write

1 Learn and trace the stroke.

横折

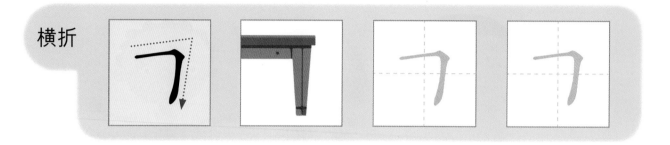

2 Learn the component. Circle 目 in the appropriate characters.

学生观察图片，引导他们发现"目"字与眼睛有关。提醒学生，"目"和"日"的区别是"目"比"日"多了一横。

3 Circle and count 目. Write the number at the centre of the target board.

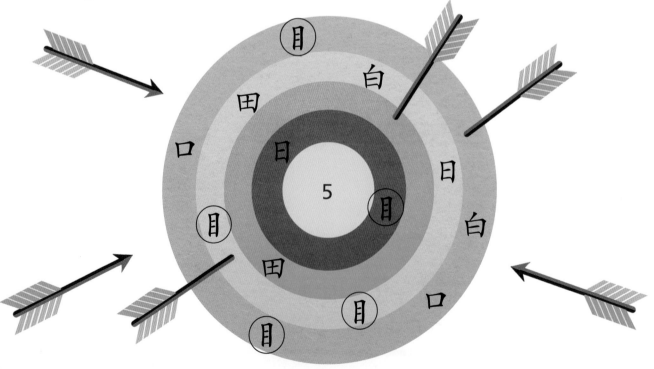

4 Trace and write the character.

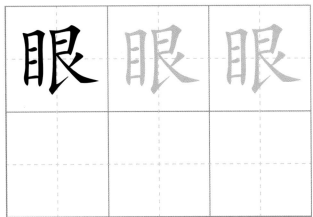

5 Write and say. 问问学生，浩浩是指着布朗尼的嘴巴、鼻子、眼睛还是耳朵。

这是小狗的  睛。

汉字小常识 Did you know?

Many components give clues to the meaning of the character.

Learn about how the characters are related to 目.

目
eye

blind

see

eyebrow

sleep

"目"是"眼睛"的意思。"盲"是指眼睛看不见，"看"是用眼睛观察，"眉"长在眼睛上方，"眠"是闭上眼睛睡觉。联系第四题，说明"眼"也是指眼睛。

多元学习 Connections

Cultures　眼保健操是根据中医理论编创的眼部按摩法。中国的小学至高中通常会在课间播放眼保健操的音乐口令，学生便跟着口令做动作，减轻眼部疲劳。

Take good care of your eyes. Learn about the Chinese eye exercises.

Eye exercises are widely practised in schools in China as a method to help students take good care of their eyes and prevent short-sightedness.

Follow the steps. Massage your eyes with your fingers.

① 双手大拇指置于右图位置旋转按压，其余手指放松，指尖抵于前额。

Under your eyebrows

② 一只手的大拇指和食指按住鼻根，再如右图上下揉捏。

Near your nose

③ 双手食指置于右图位置旋转按压，大拇指抵于下颚，其余手指自然握拳。

On your cheeks

④ 双手大拇指按太阳穴，其余手指握拳，如右图用食指侧面上下按摩眼睛周围。

Around your eyes

1 Complete the sentences. Write the letters.

看
see

a 鼻子

b 嘴巴

c 眼睛

d 耳朵

听
hear

我用 _c_ 看。

我用 _d_ 听。

闻
smell

尝
taste

我用 _a_ 闻。

我用 _b_ 尝。

2 Make funny faces with fruit and vegetables.

这是她的嘴巴。

这是他的眼睛。

这是他的耳朵。

让学生三人一组，设计作品并分别准备相应的蔬菜或水果带回学校。全班制作好作品后，轮流展示并介绍作品的脸部器官，然后比一比哪组的最有趣。提醒学生在制作时注意刀具的安全使用，并告诉他们尽量避免浪费食物，完成作品后可以将食物带回家洗净食用或用作烹调。

温习 Checkpoint

1 Answer the questions from children around the world.

提醒学生先选定一个人物，然后按顺时针或逆时针的方向依次答题，这样便不会漏答题目。

我七岁。你几岁？

我六/七/八岁。

你叫什么名字？

我叫……

What are these?

这是眼睛。

Can you say 'hello' in Chinese?

你好！

Can you write 'eye' in Chinese?

眼

这是我的嘴巴。

This is my mouth.

How do you say this in Chinese?

评核方法：

学生两人一组，互相考察评价表内单词和句子的听说读写。交际沟通部分由老师朗读要求，学生再互相对话。如果达到了某项技能要求，则用色笔将星星或小辣椒涂色。

2 Work with your friend. Colour the stars and the chillies.

Words and sentences	说	读	写
头	☆	☆	🌶
耳朵	☆	☆	🌶
眼睛	☆	☆	🌶
鼻子	☆	☆	🌶
嘴巴	☆	☆	🌶
这	☆	🌶	🌶
是	☆	🌶	🌶
的	☆	🌶	🌶
这是我的头。	☆	☆	🌶

Talk about parts of the face	☆

Can you point to my 鼻子?

Point to the girl's nose.

Can you read this sentence aloud?

这是我的爸爸和妈妈。

Can you point to my 耳朵?

Point to the boy's ears.

3 What does your teacher say?

My teacher says ...

评核建议：

根据学生课堂表现，分别给予"太棒了！(Excellent!)"、"不错！(Good!)"或"继续努力！(Work harder!)"的评价，再让学生圈出上方对应的表情，以记录自己的学习情况。

21

分享 Sharing

延伸活动：

1 学生用手遮盖英文，读中文单词，并思考单词意思；

2 学生用手遮盖中文单词，看着英文说出对应的中文单词；

3 学生三人一组，尽量运用中文单词复述第4至第9页内容。

Words I remember

头	tóu	head
耳朵	ěr duo	ear
眼睛	yǎn jing	eye
鼻子	bí zi	nose
嘴巴	zuǐ ba	mouth
这	zhè	this
是	shì	to be
的	de	of

Other words

我们	wǒ men	we, us
都	dōu	both, all
不	bù	not
一样	yī yàng	same

OXFORD

UNIVERSITY PRESS

Oxford University Press is a department of the University of Oxford.
It furthers the University's objective of excellence in research, scholarship,
and education by publishing worldwide. Oxford is a registered trade mark of
Oxford University Press in the UK and in certain other countries

Published in Hong Kong by
Oxford University Press (China) Limited
39th Floor, One Kowloon, 1 Wang Yuen Street, Kowloon Bay,
Hong Kong

Illustrated by Anne Lee and Wildman

Photographs for reproduction permitted by Dreamstime.com

China National Publications Import & Export (Group) Corporation is an authorized distributor of
Oxford Elementary Chinese.

Please contact content@cnpiec.com.cn or 86-10-65856782

ISBN: 978-0-19-082140-1

10 9 8 7 6 5 4 3 2

Teacher's Edition
ISBN: 978-0-19-082152-4

10 9 8 7 6 5 4 3 2